Connected: Understanding and Overcoming the Global Loneliness Epidemic

Connected: Understanding and Overcoming the Global Loneliness Epidemic

Sophia Newman

Copyright Page

Title: Connected: Understanding and Overcoming the Global Loneliness Epidemic

Author: Sophia Newman

Publisher: Quite Frank Educational Services
Richmond, BC, Canada

Cover Design: By the author
Printed in the United States of America

ISBN: 978-1-997668-46-6

Connected: Understanding and Overcoming the Global Loneliness Epidemic

Table of Contents

Disclaimer

This book is intended for general informational and educational purposes only. It is not a substitute for professional medical, psychological, or legal advice. Readers should consult qualified professionals regarding specific questions about their health, well-being, or circumstances.

While every effort has been made to ensure the accuracy and reliability of the information presented, the author and publisher make no representations or warranties of any kind, express or implied, about the completeness, accuracy, or suitability of this content. Any reliance you place on such information is strictly at your own risk.

The author and publisher disclaim any liability for loss, damage, or injury caused, directly or indirectly, by the use or misuse of the information in this book.

AI Acknowledgement

The research, writing, editing, and structuring of this book were supported in part by advanced AI tools. These tools were used to:

- Organize and synthesize complex research materials into accessible language.

- Assist in drafting, refining, and editing chapters.

- Generate ideas for structure, examples, and case studies.

The content was developed under the guidance, direction, and final review of the author, ensuring accuracy, coherence, and originality. All facts, interpretations, and conclusions are ultimately the responsibility of the author.

Introduction – The Ties That Bind (and Why They're Fraying)

If you've ever felt a pang of loneliness at a crowded party, you already know something profound about human connection: it's not just about being around people. It's about feeling seen, valued, and understood. And in today's world - where you can "connect" with hundreds of people without leaving your couch - those feelings are in surprisingly short supply.

We are living through what health experts now call a **global loneliness epidemic**. It's not a poetic exaggeration. According to the World Health Organization, roughly **one in six people worldwide** is experiencing loneliness at any given moment. In some countries, surveys suggest the number is closer to one in three. This isn't just a sad statistic - it's a public health warning on par with smoking, obesity, or lack of exercise. Chronic loneliness is linked to higher rates of heart disease, stroke, depression, dementia, and even premature death. The U.S. Surgeon General has gone so far as to compare its health risks to smoking fifteen cigarettes a day.

But here's the tricky part: loneliness isn't simply "being alone," and its solutions aren't as easy as "just get out and meet people." Loneliness is deeply personal and profoundly structural - an experience shaped by your inner thoughts, your relationships, your community, and the broader systems you live within. A teenager glued to their phone, an elderly widow in a rural village, and a new immigrant navigating an unfamiliar city may all feel lonely, but the roots of their loneliness - and the steps to address it - look entirely different.

Not a New Problem, But a New Urgency

The phrase "loneliness epidemic" has gained a lot of traction in the last few years, especially during and after COVID-19 lockdowns. And it's true - the pandemic intensified isolation in ways few of us had experienced before. But history tells us loneliness has been quietly building for decades, even centuries.

Social scientists have been sounding alarms for over 100 years. In the 1920s, historians described Americans as "nervous" about rapid societal changes. In the 1950s, sociologist David Riesman warned that our growing obsession with appearances and external validation was eroding genuine social bonds. By the year 2000, political scientist Robert Putnam famously documented our retreat from civic life in *Bowling Alone*, showing how declining community participation was leaving us adrift. Even before smartphones and social media, the slow unraveling of communal life was well underway.

The pandemic didn't start this fire - it just threw gasoline on it.

Why Loneliness Hits Harder Now

Modern life is a paradox. We have more tools than ever to connect, yet more people feel disconnected. Part of the problem lies in how our societies are built. Our cities, our work cultures, even our leisure activities increasingly prioritize **efficiency, individual achievement, and economic productivity** over shared experiences and mutual care. Many of the "third places" that once fostered casual human contact - cafes, libraries, local clubs - have disappeared or become less accessible. For people on the margins - those living in poverty, dealing with disabilities, or navigating cultural barriers - social connection has become a luxury rather than a basic human right.

Technology plays a double role. For some, it's a lifeline - a way to maintain friendships across continents or find community when none exists nearby. For others, especially when overused, it replaces deeper, face-to-face interactions with a steady drip of shallow connections. The result? More scrolling, fewer shared meals. More likes, less love.

Why This Book Exists

The purpose of this book is to bring the science, history, and policy of loneliness into the open - and to do so in a way that feels **human**, not just academic. The research is clear: loneliness is not just "in your head," and it's not a personal failing. It's a complex condition shaped by everything from your thought patterns to your neighborhood design, from national policies to cultural values. Addressing it requires coordinated action at every level - personal, community, and governmental.

You'll find that this book doesn't stop at diagnosing the problem. It offers practical tools, inspiring case studies, and hopeful visions of a more connected future. We'll explore why the human brain treats loneliness like a survival threat, how urban planners can design neighborhoods that spark conversation, why "social prescribing" is becoming a public health tool, and what you - yes, you - can do to strengthen your own social web.

And here's the hopeful truth: loneliness is not inevitable. Across the world, from small towns in Canada to bustling cities in Japan, from grassroots community projects to global policy shifts, people are finding ways to reconnect. The solutions are not one-size-fits-all, but they share a common thread: they recognize that human connection is as essential as food, water, and shelter.

If you've ever wished you had stronger ties, if you've wondered why our hyper-connected world feels so disconnected, or if you simply want to understand one of the most pressing public health challenges of our time - you're in the right place.

Because loneliness might be a personal feeling, but it's a shared problem. And together, we can do something about it.

Chapter 1 – The Invisible Crisis: Why Loneliness Is More Than a Feeling

Imagine this: you're in a room full of people. Music is playing, conversations are buzzing, laughter bounces off the walls - and yet, you feel like you're behind a pane of glass, watching it all happen from the outside. People see you, maybe even talk to you, but you don't feel *seen*. That strange, hollow ache? That's loneliness.

It's an experience so common that almost everyone has felt it at some point. But here's the startling truth: for millions, loneliness isn't a fleeting mood - it's a constant companion. And while it doesn't leave visible scars, its fingerprints are all over our physical health, mental well-being, and even the way our societies function.

The World Health Organization now calls loneliness a **global public health issue**. It affects roughly **one in six people worldwide**, with especially high rates among young adults and older populations. In the United States, national surveys reveal that about **half of all adults** report feeling lonely at least some of the time. In the UK, chronic loneliness affects over 7% of the population - millions of people. And this is not confined to wealthy nations; in lower-income countries, loneliness is also a growing and under-recognized problem, often exacerbated by migration, displacement, and poverty.

This chapter will peel back the layers of what loneliness actually is, why it matters so much more than we've been led to believe, and how it has quietly transformed from a private discomfort into a collective crisis.

Loneliness Is Not Just "Being Alone"

One of the biggest misconceptions about loneliness is that it's simply about physical solitude. If that were true, the cure would be easy: just be around more people. But loneliness is **subjective** - it's the gap between the social connections you *want* and the ones you *have*.

You can be surrounded by friends at a dinner party and still feel profoundly lonely if the interactions don't feel meaningful. On the flip side, someone who spends long stretches alone might feel perfectly content if their need for connection is being met through a few deep, high-quality relationships.

Researchers draw a sharp line between two related but distinct concepts:

- **Loneliness**: A subjective, emotional response to a perceived lack of social connection.

- **Social Isolation**: An objective state of having few social contacts or relationships, regardless of how you feel about it.

Why does this matter? Because someone can be socially isolated without feeling lonely, and vice versa. Treating these as interchangeable leads to ineffective solutions. A person who feels lonely despite having an active social calendar doesn't necessarily need *more* social interaction - they need *better* social interaction.

Why Loneliness Matters for Your Health

It might sound dramatic to say that loneliness can kill you - but the science says it's true. In fact, the health risks of chronic loneliness are **on par with smoking, obesity, and physical inactivity**.

Studies have shown that loneliness and social isolation:

- Increase the risk of **premature death** by up to 29%.

- Raise the risk of **heart disease** by 29% and **stroke** by 32%.

- Heighten the risk of developing **dementia** in older adults by up to 50%.

- Contribute to a higher likelihood of **depression, anxiety, and suicidality**.

Why would something as intangible as loneliness have such tangible, dangerous effects? The answer lies in our evolutionary wiring. For most of human history, isolation was dangerous - being cut off from your group could mean starvation, predation, or death. Our brains evolved to treat disconnection as a survival threat, triggering stress responses meant to keep us alert and vigilant.

The problem? In the modern world, that survival mode doesn't turn off when isolation is prolonged. Instead, it batters the body with chronic stress hormones, disrupts sleep, fuels inflammation, and erodes immune function. Over time, this constant state of alertness wears down the heart, the brain, and the body's ability to repair itself.

A Crisis That Crosses Borders and Ages

Loneliness is both universal and uneven. It exists in every culture, but it doesn't affect everyone equally. Globally, prevalence hovers around 16% at any given time, but certain groups experience it more intensely:

- **Adolescents and young adults**: Social media, academic pressure, and life transitions create a perfect storm for disconnection, even amid constant digital "contact."

- **Older adults**: Loss of partners and friends, declining health, reduced mobility, and retirement all contribute to shrinking social networks.

- **Low-income individuals**: Economic stress, "time poverty" from multiple jobs, and lack of access to social spaces deepen isolation.

- **Immigrants and marginalized communities**: Cultural barriers, discrimination, and the absence of familiar support networks can intensify feelings of exclusion.

The fact that loneliness follows a **U-shaped curve** - hitting hardest in early adulthood and again in later life - challenges the stereotype that it's just an "old person's problem." In reality, the causes, consequences, and solutions vary widely depending on life stage.

Why It's an "Epidemic"

The word "epidemic" is usually reserved for infectious diseases, but public health experts are increasingly using it to describe social conditions that spread widely and have serious health impacts. In the case of loneliness, the analogy works in more ways than one:

- **It's widespread**: Like a contagious illness, loneliness can ripple through communities. Research shows it can spread through social networks - if your friends are lonely, your own risk increases.

- **It's harmful**: The health risks are as severe as many diseases.

- **It's preventable**: With the right interventions, loneliness can be reduced, and the health impacts mitigated.

In June 2025, the World Health Assembly passed its **first-ever resolution** declaring social connection a global health priority, following the release of the WHO's flagship report on the issue. This was a landmark moment - an official acknowledgment that disconnection isn't just a personal challenge but a societal threat.

The Vicious Cycles of Disconnection

One of the reasons loneliness is so difficult to address is that it feeds on itself. Psychologists call these **maladaptive cycles**:

1. **Negative social expectations**: You anticipate rejection, so you withdraw.

2. **Reduced interaction**: With fewer opportunities for connection, your fears seem confirmed.

3. **Heightened vigilance**: You become more sensitive to signs of exclusion.

4. **Deeper isolation**: The less you connect, the harder it becomes to try again.

These cycles can be broken, but doing so often requires both personal effort and systemic change - a theme that will run throughout this book.

Not Just a Feeling - A Societal Mirror

If we zoom out from the personal experience of loneliness, we start to see it as a reflection of the societies we live in. Over the last century, economic and cultural shifts have reshaped how we live, work, and interact.

- **Urban design** has often prioritized cars over community, creating environments where casual human contact is rare.

- **Workplace culture** in many countries prizes productivity over well-being, leaving little time for social life.

- **Technology** has simultaneously expanded our reach and thinned the depth of our relationships.

Loneliness, in this light, isn't just a byproduct of individual circumstances - it's a symptom of broader social architecture. That means fixing it will require rethinking how we design cities, structure work, regulate technology, and support community spaces.

Where We Go from Here

The invisibility of loneliness makes it easy to dismiss. There's no rash, no fever, no X-ray to diagnose it. But its effects are measurable in hospital admissions, mental health crises, and even death rates. Left unaddressed, it chips away at both individual lives and collective resilience.

In the chapters ahead, we'll explore loneliness from every angle - its biological roots, its cultural history, its uneven distribution, and the ways it intersects with economics, technology, and urban planning. We'll also highlight interventions that are working, from **cognitive-behavioral therapy** for reframing social fears to **social prescribing** programs that connect people with community groups, arts activities, or volunteering opportunities.

And most importantly, we'll remind ourselves that while loneliness is deeply personal, it's never just yours to bear alone. Connection is a shared human need - and building it back is a shared human responsibility.

If you're ready, Chapter 2 will take us deeper into **the roots of the problem** - how our economic systems, cultural values, and physical environments have been quietly shaping the modern loneliness epidemic for generations.

Chapter 2 – The Complex Roots of Social Disconnection

If loneliness were just a matter of having too few friends or not enough time to socialize, the fix would be straightforward: make more friends, spend more time together. But the reality is far more complicated. Loneliness is woven into the fabric of modern life - not just in our personal habits, but in the way our societies are structured, our economies function, and even the physical spaces we inhabit.

This chapter looks under the hood of the "loneliness epidemic" to explore its deep roots. We'll see that while individual choices matter, many of the forces pulling us apart are systemic, baked into the rhythms of 21st-century life.

The Social Order: When Individualism Comes at a Cost

In much of the modern West, the cultural script celebrates **individualism** - self-reliance, personal achievement, and the idea that we should all be the authors of our own lives. There's a lot to admire in this philosophy: it can fuel ambition, encourage creativity, and protect personal freedoms. But taken too far, it has a hidden cost: the slow erosion of the communal bonds that humans have relied on for survival for millennia.

Historically, communities were bound together by necessity. You didn't just know your neighbors - you needed them. They were your safety net, your workforce, your entertainment, and your emergency service all rolled into one. In an age of global supply chains, on-demand services, and portable careers, we *can* survive without leaning on each other - but that independence can quietly turn into isolation.

Capitalism has added another twist. In a market-driven world, relationships can start to feel transactional. From LinkedIn networking to dating app swipes, human connections can be reduced to profiles, resumes, and quick judgments. The very platforms designed to connect us often turn us into commodities, packaging our personalities into neat little digital "profiles" that can be browsed and discarded in seconds.

It's not just romantic or professional relationships that are affected. Consumer culture, which thrives on constant desire and dissatisfaction, often encourages people to fill emotional gaps with purchases rather than people. Theodor Adorno, a 20th-century social critic, called this the "standardization of culture" - a world where individuality is an illusion, and where genuine connection is replaced by mass-produced substitutes.

When Time Itself Becomes a Barrier

For people at the lower end of the income ladder, loneliness often has less to do with choice and more to do with **time poverty**. If you're juggling multiple jobs with unpredictable schedules, finding the time - or the energy - to maintain friendships can feel impossible. Social gatherings, volunteering, even casual coffee meetups become luxuries you simply can't afford.

Chronic financial stress also chips away at the emotional bandwidth needed for connection. Depression rates are higher among those experiencing economic hardship, and depression, in turn, tends to make social engagement harder. This creates a vicious cycle: financial strain reduces connection, and reduced connection makes it harder to cope with financial strain.

The result is a society where social connection increasingly feels like a privilege - one that's unevenly distributed along lines of class, education, and access.

The Digital Paradox: Connected Yet Alone

If there's one arena where the loneliness conversation gets heated, it's technology. Is it saving us from isolation, or making it worse? The answer is… both.

On the plus side, digital tools can bridge physical distance, maintain long-distance relationships, and create communities for people who might otherwise be isolated - think of LGBTQ+ youth in rural areas finding support online, or older adults using video calls to keep up with grandchildren. This is known as the **stimulation hypothesis**: technology can enhance and expand our existing social connections.

But there's a darker side, summed up by the **displacement hypothesis**. Time spent online - especially on social media - can replace deeper, in-person interactions. The more we scroll, the less we may engage face-to-face. And unlike a conversation over coffee, a "like" on a photo doesn't lower blood pressure, reduce stress hormones, or boost immune function the way real-time, physical social contact can.

The relationship between tech use and loneliness isn't one-directional. People who already feel lonely may turn to digital platforms for connection, but excessive online time can deepen isolation, creating a self-reinforcing cycle. In other words, the lonelier you feel, the more likely you are to seek solace online - and the more time you spend online, the lonelier you may become.

This doesn't mean technology is inherently harmful. The difference lies in how it's used. A video chat with an old friend across the country is a world apart from hours of passive scrolling through strangers' highlight reels.

The Role of Place: How Our Environments Shape Connection

The spaces we inhabit - our neighborhoods, cities, and public areas - aren't just backdrops to our social lives. They actively shape how, when, and whether we connect with others.

Urban planners talk about **"third places"** - informal gathering spots like cafes, parks, libraries, and community centers. These spaces foster casual, low-stakes interactions that help build a sense of belonging. But in many cities, these places are disappearing or becoming less accessible due to rising rents, privatization, or a focus on car-oriented development.

When communities are designed around cars rather than pedestrians, people lose the everyday encounters - chatting with a shop owner, waving to a neighbor - that form the "weak ties" crucial to social networks. Add to this the spread of suburban sprawl, where homes are far apart and amenities aren't within walking distance, and opportunities for connection shrink dramatically.

Some cities are pushing back. **Transit-based urbanism** - designing neighborhoods around public transport hubs - puts essential services and social spaces within walking or biking distance, making it easier for people to bump into one another naturally. Groups like *The Loneliness Lab* advocate for embedding "design for connection" into urban planning, from wide sidewalks to park benches to community gardens.

In rural areas, the challenge is often the reverse: vast distances and limited public transportation mean social opportunities are physically out of reach for those without reliable mobility.

The Pandemic Accelerator

While loneliness has been building for decades, the COVID-19 pandemic acted like a giant magnifying glass, enlarging every crack in our social infrastructure. Lockdowns severed casual connections overnight, while fear of infection turned once-normal activities - like sharing a meal or attending a concert - into potential health risks.

For some, the shift to remote work offered flexibility and relief from long commutes. For others, it meant the loss of their main source of daily human interaction. The effects weren't evenly distributed - older adults, people with disabilities, and those without access to digital technology often experienced the steepest declines in connection.

The pandemic didn't invent loneliness, but it stripped away the coping mechanisms many relied on, forcing the problem into public view.

Structural Problems Need Structural Solutions

One of the key takeaways from global research is that you can't "self-help" your way out of a systemic problem. Yes, individual strategies - like practicing social skills, volunteering, or limiting passive screen time - are valuable. But when loneliness is rooted in work schedules, housing design, economic policy, or the architecture of digital platforms, personal effort can only go so far.

If your neighborhood has no safe public spaces, your income keeps you working two jobs, and public transport is unreliable, "just go make friends" is more a slogan than a solution. Real change will require what experts call **social-ecological strategies** - interventions that operate at the personal, community, and policy levels all at once.

Why Understanding the Roots Matters

If loneliness is a tree, personal feelings are the leaves - but the roots are deep, tangled, and hidden underground. We can trim the leaves all we want, but unless we address what's feeding the roots - economic inequality, the commodification of relationships, the loss of public gathering spaces, the way our cities are built - we'll keep seeing the same symptoms year after year.

Understanding the structural drivers doesn't just help policymakers - it also helps us show ourselves a little compassion. If you've been feeling disconnected, it's not simply because you're "bad at making friends" or "too introverted." It may be because you're living in a society that makes connection harder than it should be.

From Awareness to Action

The good news? Many of these structural problems are solvable. Cities can be redesigned to encourage interaction. Workplaces can be structured to promote real community instead of isolated competition. Digital tools can be regulated and reimagined to support deep, meaningful communication.

But the first step is understanding that loneliness isn't just an individual's burden - it's a societal challenge. And societal challenges require collective action.

In **Chapter 3**, we'll dive into the human body and mind to explore **"Disorders of the Loneliness Kind"** - the biological, psychological, and cognitive consequences of chronic loneliness. You'll see how disconnection can quite literally change the brain, alter the immune system, and shape long-term health outcomes.

Chapter 3 – "Disorders of the Loneliness Kind"

When most people think of loneliness, they picture an emotional ache - a sense of emptiness or longing for connection. But researchers now know that loneliness doesn't just *feel* bad. It's a whole-body experience with measurable effects on our hearts, brains, immune systems, and even our genes. Chronic loneliness is not simply "all in your head" - it is also in your blood pressure, your inflammatory markers, and your brain chemistry.

The phrase **"Disorders of the Loneliness Kind"** comes from the growing recognition that persistent social disconnection is as damaging to our health as some of the most well-known risk factors for disease. In fact, the U.S. Surgeon General has compared the health risks of being socially disconnected to smoking **up to fifteen cigarettes a day**.

This chapter will explore what loneliness does to the body, the mind, and the very cells that keep us alive.

The Body Under Siege

One of the clearest findings from decades of research is that loneliness **shortens lives**. Large-scale studies have found that chronic loneliness and social isolation:

- Increase the risk of **premature death** by up to 29%.

- Raise the likelihood of **heart disease** by 29% and **stroke** by 32%.

- Heighten the risk of developing **dementia** in older adults by about 50%.

These numbers are not abstract. They mean that loneliness belongs in the same public health conversation as smoking, obesity, and high blood pressure.

Why does it hit the cardiovascular system so hard? One reason is that loneliness activates the body's **stress response** - the "fight or flight" system that evolved to protect us from predators and danger. The problem is that the body reacts to *social* threats - like feeling excluded - almost as if they were *physical* threats.

When that stress system is constantly triggered, heart rate and blood pressure stay elevated, blood vessels become damaged, and the immune system shifts into a pro-inflammatory state. Over time, this contributes to atherosclerosis (the buildup of plaque in arteries), increases the risk of clotting, and makes the heart more vulnerable to disease.

Animal studies back this up: socially isolated animals develop more arterial plaque than those living in groups. The takeaway is clear - connection isn't just nice to have; it's cardioprotective.

The Mind in Retreat

Loneliness isn't just hard on the heart - it takes a heavy toll on the mind.

Psychologists describe loneliness and depression as a **two-way street**. Feeling disconnected can lead to depressive symptoms, and depression can make it harder to seek out connection, creating a **vicious cycle**:

1. **Loneliness triggers low mood** and feelings of worthlessness.

2. **Low mood leads to withdrawal**, making social contact even rarer.

3. **Withdrawal deepens loneliness**, and the cycle repeats.

This loop is particularly dangerous because loneliness also increases the risk of **anxiety, self-harm**, and **suicidality**. Some studies suggest that lonely adults are more than twice as likely to develop depression compared to those who feel socially connected.

For older adults, the stakes are even higher. Loneliness is associated with faster cognitive decline - including memory loss, reduced mental processing speed, and poorer problem-solving abilities. It is also linked to a significantly increased risk of Alzheimer's and other dementias.

One theory is that loneliness may be a **prodromal stage** of dementia - a sign that brain changes are already underway before full-blown symptoms appear. Another theory suggests that the lack of social stimulation directly weakens the neural pathways involved in memory, language, and reasoning.

Social Pain and Physical Pain: The Brain's Confusion

One of the most fascinating discoveries in neuroscience is that the brain processes **social pain** and **physical pain** in remarkably similar ways.

When people experience social rejection or exclusion, brain scans show increased activity in the **dorsal anterior cingulate cortex** and the **anterior insula** - regions that also light up when we feel physical pain. This overlap may explain why we use the same language for both experiences: "hurt feelings," "broken heart," "emotional wounds."

Even more intriguing, one study found that taking acetaminophen (Tylenol) reduced self-reported feelings of social pain and lowered activity in these pain-related brain areas. This doesn't mean loneliness can be solved with a pill - but it does show that our brains treat social exclusion as a real, physical injury.

The Immune System's Misguided Defense

From an evolutionary standpoint, being alone in the wild meant greater vulnerability to injury and attack. To prepare for this, the body developed a defensive strategy: ramp up inflammation (to heal potential wounds) and temporarily downregulate antiviral responses (since viruses spread more easily in groups).

In modern life, this same ancient survival mechanism kicks in when we feel socially disconnected - except now, it's a harmful mismatch. Chronic loneliness triggers a persistent **low-grade inflammatory state**, marked by elevated levels of molecules like CRP and IL-6.

At the same time, the antiviral response is weakened. This makes lonely individuals more susceptible to infections like the flu - and even when they do get sick, their bodies are slower to recover. Long-term inflammation, meanwhile, becomes "molecular fuel" for chronic illnesses such as cardiovascular disease, diabetes, Alzheimer's, and certain cancers.

Behavioral Pathways: How Loneliness Changes Habits

It's not just biology - loneliness also influences behavior in ways that worsen health risks:

- **Poor sleep**: Lonely individuals often experience fragmented or restless sleep, which impairs immune function and mood regulation.

- **Less exercise**: Without social encouragement or shared activities, physical activity often declines.

- **Unhealthy coping**: Increased alcohol consumption, smoking, or overeating are common self-soothing strategies that carry long-term health costs.

In short, loneliness makes it harder to take care of yourself, and poor self-care reinforces loneliness - a self-reinforcing loop similar to the depression cycle.

The Downstream Consequences for Society

When millions of people are chronically lonely, the ripple effects reach far beyond individual health. Healthcare systems bear the cost of increased hospital visits, longer recovery times, and higher rates of chronic illness. Economies lose productivity when employees disengage or take more sick days.

There's also the social cost: loneliness can undermine trust, weaken community resilience, and even shape political polarization. When people feel alienated, they are less likely to participate in civic life, less inclined to help strangers, and more vulnerable to extremist narratives that promise belonging.

Breaking the Biological and Psychological Loops

The good news is that the biological and psychological effects of loneliness are not set in stone. Studies show that **targeted interventions** - from cognitive-behavioral therapy (CBT) to group-based activities - can reduce loneliness and its associated health risks.

CBT, for instance, works by addressing the **negative attribution biases** that keep people stuck in avoidance mode ("They probably don't want to talk to me" becomes "Maybe they're just busy"). Behavioral activation encourages people to engage in rewarding activities that bring a sense of accomplishment and social contact.

On the biological side, regular exercise, better sleep, and stress reduction can help reset the body's overactive stress and inflammation responses - especially when these habits are built into a supportive community context.

Why This Science Matters

Understanding the biopsychosocial impact of loneliness reframes it from a "soft" problem to a **serious public health issue**. You wouldn't tell someone with high blood pressure to "just relax," and we shouldn't tell someone who is lonely to "just get out more" without recognizing the deeper changes happening in their body and brain.

When policymakers, healthcare providers, and communities understand that loneliness is as physiologically real as heart disease, the case for large-scale action becomes undeniable.

In Chapter 4, we'll look at exactly what those actions can be. We'll explore a **multi-tiered framework** for intervention - one that spans the personal, community, and policy levels, drawing on successful models from around the world and showing how they can be adapted to different contexts.

Chapter 4 – A Multi-Tiered Framework for Intervention

By now, it's clear: loneliness isn't just an emotional state you "snap out of." It's a complex public health challenge with roots in psychology, biology, social structures, and policy. And like any complex problem, it won't be solved with a single, magic-bullet fix.

The good news is that researchers and policymakers have been busy designing and testing solutions. The result is a **multi-tiered framework** - a strategy that works on three interconnected levels:

1. **Individual and clinical approaches** (helping people directly).

2. **Community and institutional initiatives** (strengthening the local web of connection).

3. **Governmental and policy responses** (changing the conditions that shape how we live).

Think of it as gardening. You don't just water the plant (individual help); you also make sure the soil is healthy (community support) and the climate is favorable (policies and infrastructure). All three have to work together.

Level 1: Individual and Clinical Strategies

At the personal level, interventions aim to equip people with the tools, skills, and support to break out of the cycles that loneliness can create. These are often delivered through healthcare or mental health settings, but many can be self-initiated.

Cognitive-Behavioral Therapy (CBT)

CBT has one of the strongest evidence bases for reducing loneliness. It tackles the unhelpful thought patterns that can make social interaction feel risky or pointless. For example:

- **Before CBT**: "If I reach out, they'll probably ignore me."
- **After CBT**: "Maybe they're busy, but it's worth trying - I've enjoyed our chats before."

CBT also uses **behavioral experiments**, where people gradually test new social behaviors in low-pressure settings, building confidence over time.

Social Skills Training (SST)

Sometimes loneliness isn't about negative thinking - it's about lacking the skills to connect comfortably. SST teaches the practical "micro-skills" of conversation and interaction:

- How to ask open-ended questions.
- How to read nonverbal cues.
- How to join group activities without feeling intrusive.

When SST is paired with CBT, people not only think more positively about connection but also have the tools to make it happen.

Self-Care and Lifestyle Interventions

Healthy routines can buffer against the mental and physical effects of loneliness. Regular exercise, adequate sleep, balanced nutrition, and mindfulness practices like meditation improve emotional resilience, making social engagement easier.

Even small steps - like taking a daily walk in a park where you might see familiar faces - can have cumulative benefits.

Volunteering and Purpose-Driven Activities

Helping others is a surprisingly powerful antidote to loneliness. It provides both structure and meaning, while also creating opportunities for organic connection. From mentoring students to walking dogs at an animal shelter, purpose-driven activities can turn social contact into something deeply rewarding.

Level 2: Community and Institutional Initiatives

Even the most motivated individual will struggle if their surroundings are hostile to connection. This is where community-based solutions come in - designed to make everyday social contact more natural and accessible.

Social Prescribing

Pioneered in the UK and now spreading globally, social prescribing allows healthcare providers to "prescribe" non-medical interventions like art classes, walking groups, or gardening clubs. Patients are connected to **link workers** who guide them toward activities suited to their interests and needs.

The benefits are twofold: people get meaningful engagement, and healthcare systems see reduced demand for services that were previously addressing loneliness-related symptoms indirectly.

Third Places and Public Spaces

Parks, libraries, cafes, and community centers are vital infrastructure for connection. But they require investment and intentional design:

- **Affordability**: Free or low-cost access encourages diverse participation.

- **Proximity**: Spaces need to be close enough for people to reach without major effort.

- **Programming**: Events, workshops, and drop-in activities keep spaces active and inviting.

Innovative examples include:

- **The Dutch "Chat Checkout"**: Grocery store lanes for customers who want to have a friendly conversation with the cashier.

- **Japan's intergenerational care centers**: Facilities that combine daycare for children with social spaces for older adults, encouraging daily cross-generational contact.

Workplace Connection Programs

For many adults, work is the main source of daily human interaction. Yet surveys show a growing number of employees feel isolated at work. Solutions include:

- Mentorship programs that pair new hires with experienced staff.

- "Walk and talk" meetings that combine discussion with movement.

- Flexible spaces that encourage casual conversation instead of siloed work.

A connected workplace isn't just nice - it's linked to higher job satisfaction, lower turnover, and better mental health.

Level 3: Governmental and Policy Responses

This is where the "climate" for connection is set. Governments can either create conditions that make connection easier - or inadvertently make it harder. The most effective national strategies take a **"Connection-in-All-Policies"** approach, evaluating the social impact of decisions in sectors like housing, transportation, and technology.

Appointing National Leadership

The UK's creation of a **Minister for Loneliness** in 2018 signaled that social connection was a matter of state-level importance. Similar roles in other countries could coordinate cross-sector efforts and ensure policies are aligned.

Infrastructure Investments

- **Urban planning**: Designing neighborhoods around public transport and walkability increases casual interactions.

- **Digital inclusion**: Providing internet access and training for older adults ensures they're not left out of modern communication channels.

- **Affordable transportation**: Subsidized or free transit helps people reach social activities.

Health Sector Mobilization

Training healthcare workers to screen for loneliness - and giving them referral pathways to community resources - integrates social health into routine care. This approach is already being piloted in parts of Canada, the UK, and Japan.

Reforming Digital Environments

Governments can work with tech companies to:

- Improve data transparency on the mental health impacts of social media.

- Encourage platform designs that foster meaningful interaction rather than passive scrolling.

- Support digital tools that complement, rather than replace, offline contact.

Bringing It All Together

The power of the multi-tiered approach is that it recognizes loneliness as **both a personal experience and a societal design issue**.

For example:

- An older adult feeling isolated (Level 1) might benefit from CBT and a social prescribing referral.

- That referral leads to a community center program (Level 2) located in a walkable neighborhood funded through urban planning policy (Level 3).

By addressing multiple layers at once, we not only help individuals but also reshape the environment to make connection easier for everyone.

Measuring Success

We can't improve what we don't measure. Effective loneliness strategies track:

1. **Loneliness scores** (using tools like the UCLA-3 scale).

2. **Connection metrics** (quality and quantity of supportive ties).

3. **Health utilization** (ER visits, primary care use).

4. **Functional outcomes** (work or school attendance).

5. **Equity measures** (are improvements happening across all demographics?).

From Theory to Action

The multi-tiered framework isn't just a public health theory - it's a practical roadmap already in motion. Countries like the UK, Japan, and Canada are showing that with political will, cultural buy-in, and smart investment, we can make connection the norm rather than the exception.

In Chapter 5, we'll explore **how capitalism and consumer culture shape the modern loneliness landscape**, digging deeper into the economic and cultural currents that push us toward isolation - and what can be done to counteract them.

Chapter 5 – A System Built for Separation

If loneliness is a personal ache, then the society we live in often works - consciously or not - to make that ache sharper. Behind the statistics and individual stories lies a bigger truth: modern economic and cultural systems are structured in ways that chip away at the foundations of connection.

This isn't about blaming "the system" for every missed dinner or quiet weekend. It's about recognizing how **structural forces** - from the way we work, to how we shop, to where we live - create conditions where loneliness can take root and flourish.

The Long Shadow of Individualism

The Western ideal of **individualism** is a double-edged sword. On one side, it celebrates personal freedom, ambition, and the right to carve out your own path. On the other, it can subtly undermine the communal bonds that make life meaningful.

Historically, communities operated on interdependence. Your neighbors weren't just friendly faces - they were your safety net, your emergency responders, and your social calendar. Now, the cultural emphasis on self-reliance often discourages asking for help or offering it.

Over time, this shift turns "We're in this together" into "You're on your own." It's no coincidence that in countries with stronger collectivist traditions - where community responsibilities are emphasized - reported rates of loneliness tend to be lower, even in densely populated cities.

Capitalism and the Commodification of Relationships

Capitalism's influence on our social lives goes deeper than simply making us work long hours. It also shapes how we view relationships themselves. In the digital age, human connection is often **packaged, marketed, and consumed** like a product.

Think about:

- **Dating apps** that turn potential partners into swipeable cards.

- **Networking platforms** where friendships blur with career advancement.

- **Influencer culture** where relationships become public-facing performances.

These systems encourage quick judgments based on surface impressions, reducing the likelihood of slower, deeper connections. And just like fast food, fast relationships can leave us feeling unsatisfied and hungry for more.

The Consumer Culture Trap

Modern consumer culture thrives on **manufactured dissatisfaction**. Advertising tells us we're incomplete without the latest phone, outfit, or gadget. The "solution" to that emptiness? Buy something.

But when emotional needs are consistently redirected toward material consumption, the underlying hunger for connection remains unaddressed. Over time, we get used to chasing the short-lived dopamine hit of a purchase rather than the slower, steadier satisfaction of a strong relationship.

Social critic Theodor Adorno argued that mass culture standardizes experiences, creating the illusion of choice while keeping us in a cycle of consumption. The result: people remain "connected" through shared consumer habits - streaming the same shows, wearing the same brands - but not necessarily through meaningful interpersonal bonds.

Work Patterns and Time Poverty

For many, work has shifted from being a means to support life to being life itself. In low-wage sectors, unstable schedules and multiple jobs create **time poverty** - not enough hours left in the day for rest, let alone for building relationships.

For higher-income workers, the issue may be **work encroachment** - always-on expectations driven by email, messaging apps, and remote work technology. Even leisure time can feel like a guilt-inducing luxury.

The irony is that workplaces could be powerful hubs for connection. But when efficiency and productivity are prioritized above all else, informal socializing gets squeezed out. Lunch breaks vanish. Water cooler chats are replaced by Slack messages. The result? Colleagues become task partners rather than genuine friends.

The Gig Economy's Isolation

The rise of gig and freelance work offers flexibility but often at the cost of community. Without a regular team or shared workspace, gig workers miss out on the small, daily interactions that build social capital.

And unlike traditional employment, gig work rarely comes with built-in opportunities for mentorship, camaraderie, or professional development - further weakening the "weak ties" that can lead to both career opportunities and a sense of belonging.

Economic Inequality and Social Segregation

Loneliness doesn't fall evenly across society - it's more common in low-income communities. The reasons are both practical and psychological:

- **Limited access to social spaces**: Membership fees, transportation costs, and neighborhood safety all influence whether people can engage socially.

- **Chronic stress**: Financial strain increases anxiety and depression, making socializing feel draining rather than restorative.

- **Stigma**: Poverty can create feelings of shame, which may discourage people from seeking connection.

Inequality also fuels **social segregation** - wealthy and low-income residents often live in different neighborhoods, attend different schools, and use different public spaces. This reduces the diversity and density of social networks, leading to more fragmented communities.

Housing and the Decline of "Third Places"

Affordable housing shortages have pushed many into transient living situations - short-term rentals, shared accommodations, or frequent moves for work. Constant relocation disrupts social networks before they have time to deepen.

At the same time, the public "third places" that once served as community anchors - cafes, bookstores, parks - are disappearing or being privatized. Rising rents force small businesses out, while public spaces are often underfunded or designed in ways that discourage lingering.

Without these casual meeting grounds, our opportunities for **low-stakes, repeated encounters** shrink dramatically. And it's those small, recurring interactions - a nod to a familiar face, a shared joke at the bus stop - that form the connective tissue of community.

Urban Design and the Geography of Isolation

Our built environment shapes our social behavior. Many modern cities are designed for cars, not people, leading to:

- Fewer pedestrian interactions.

- Longer commutes that eat into social time.

- Neighborhoods where services are spread far apart, reducing chance encounters.

Compare this with **transit-based urbanism**, where housing, shops, and public spaces cluster around transport hubs. In these environments, people naturally cross paths more often, creating both planned and spontaneous opportunities for connection.

Technology: Amplifier or Barrier?

Technology deserves its own chapter (and we'll give it one), but it's worth noting here how it interacts with economic and cultural forces. For example:

- Social media can make relationships feel transactional, mirroring capitalist logic.

- Online retail reduces the need for in-person shopping, removing casual social contact from daily life.

- Remote work platforms can weaken workplace culture when not paired with intentional community-building efforts.

The result is a strange paradox: we have more ways to "connect" than ever before, but fewer opportunities to **connect meaningfully**.

Breaking the Cycle

If modern economic systems contribute to loneliness, can they also be reimagined to reduce it? The answer is yes - but it requires intention and creativity.

Some possibilities:

- **Shorter workweeks**: More free time for social activities without loss of productivity.

- **Mixed-income housing**: Reducing social segregation and increasing neighborhood diversity.

- **Investment in public spaces**: Parks, libraries, and cultural centers as "connection infrastructure."

- **Cooperative business models**: Structuring work environments to foster collaboration and mutual support.

- **Corporate wellness programs** that go beyond gym memberships to include social clubs, volunteering, and team-building.

Why This Matters for the Next Chapters

Understanding how capitalism, consumerism, and inequality contribute to loneliness isn't about abandoning economic growth or rejecting technology. It's about **designing systems that work for human well-being, not against it**.

When policies, workplaces, and neighborhoods are built with connection in mind, the benefits spill into every area of life - better health, stronger communities, and more resilient economies.

In Chapter 6, we'll focus on **technology's double-edged role** in the loneliness epidemic - how it can both build bridges and burn them, and what it takes to ensure our digital tools help rather than harm our social health.

Chapter 6 – The Technology Trap: Connected Yet Alone

When the internet first entered everyday life, it arrived with a promise: instant communication, unlimited information, and the ability to stay close to the people who mattered most - no matter where they lived. In many ways, it has delivered on that promise. We can send a video of our child's first steps across the globe in seconds, reconnect with childhood friends on social media, or join an online group for any niche interest imaginable.

And yet, despite being more "connected" than any generation before us, loneliness has become a defining public health issue of our time. How did we get here? The answer lies in a paradox: **technology can both relieve and intensify loneliness, depending on how - and why - we use it**.

Two Hypotheses, One Complicated Reality

Researchers often frame the technology–loneliness relationship through two competing hypotheses:

1. **The Stimulation Hypothesis**
   Technology can enhance existing relationships and create new ones. Video calls, group chats, and online communities can stimulate meaningful interaction, especially for people who are geographically isolated or socially marginalized.

2. **The Displacement Hypothesis**
   Excessive screen time can replace in-person interactions. Hours spent scrolling, gaming, or messaging can crowd out opportunities for face-to-face connection, reducing both the quality and depth of social bonds.

The truth is, both hypotheses are valid - and they often operate at the same time. Technology is a tool. Whether it connects or isolates us depends on the context and intention behind its use.

When Technology Connects

There are countless examples of technology serving as a lifeline:

- **Long-Distance Relationships**: Video calls and instant messaging can help couples, families, and friends maintain intimacy across continents.

- **Support for Marginalized Groups**: LGBTQ+ youth in unsupportive environments often find acceptance and friendship in online communities.

- **Access for Older Adults**: When mobility or health limits travel, social media and messaging apps can keep older adults engaged with loved ones.

- **Shared Experiences**: Multiplayer games, livestream events, and collaborative projects can foster genuine bonds among people who may never meet in person.

In these cases, digital connection isn't a substitute for "real" interaction - it's a necessary bridge.

When Technology Divides

But the same tools that connect us can also deepen disconnection:

- **Passive Scrolling**: Consuming endless updates without meaningful interaction can trigger social comparison, leaving users feeling inadequate or excluded.

- **Shallow Interactions**: "Likes" and emoji reactions are quick to give but rarely provide the depth of face-to-face conversations.

- **Algorithmic Isolation**: Recommendation algorithms often feed users content that reinforces their existing views and social bubbles, limiting exposure to diverse perspectives and reducing common ground.

- **Addictive Design**: Many platforms are engineered for maximum engagement, rewarding users with dopamine hits for repetitive checking, which can displace time spent on more fulfilling activities.

The result? We can spend hours "socializing" online without forming any meaningful connections - like eating fast food for every meal and wondering why we're still hungry.

The Bidirectional Loop

One of the most important insights from research is that the relationship between technology use and loneliness is **bidirectional**:

- **Loneliness → More Online Time**: People who feel disconnected may turn to social media or online games to fill the gap.

- **More Online Time → More Loneliness**: If that online engagement is shallow or replaces in-person contact, it can increase feelings of isolation.

This loop is particularly common among adolescents and young adults, who are more likely to prefer digital interactions to physical ones and more susceptible to compulsive use patterns.

Digital Life Across Generations

Different age groups use technology - and are affected by it - in distinct ways:

- **Adolescents**: Heavy social media use is associated with both increased connection and increased loneliness, depending on how it's used. Peer validation can be powerful, but online bullying and social comparison are real risks.

- **Young Adults**: Technology can help maintain far-flung friendships during transitional life stages (college, early career), but reliance on digital contact can hinder the development of local support networks.

- **Older Adults**: Digital literacy programs can reduce loneliness in older populations by enabling them to communicate with family and join online communities. However, lack of access or confidence with technology can exacerbate isolation.

The Pandemic's Digital Stress Test

The COVID-19 pandemic forced a massive, real-time experiment in online living. For months, technology was the primary - or only - channel for social interaction for billions of people.

For some, it was a lifesaver: virtual happy hours, online classes, and video family dinners kept connections alive. For others, the lack of physical presence led to "Zoom fatigue," a sense of emotional exhaustion from constant screen-mediated interaction.

The pandemic revealed a key truth: **digital tools can maintain existing relationships, but they struggle to replace the serendipity, nuance, and intimacy of in-person contact**.

Design Matters: Tech as Public Health Infrastructure

If we think of technology as part of our social environment - like roads, parks, or libraries - it becomes clear that design choices have public health consequences.

Possible pro-connection design features include:

- **Small Group Spaces**: Tools that prioritize small, focused interactions over large, anonymous feeds.

- **Intentional Friction**: Features that encourage reflection before posting or limit endless scrolling.

- **Community Moderation**: Systems that promote respectful dialogue and minimize harassment.

- **Offline Encouragement**: Prompts to take conversations offline or meet in person when possible.

On the flip side, designs that maximize engagement time without regard to interaction quality can inadvertently fuel the loneliness epidemic.

Digital Literacy as a Social Skill

Just as healthy eating requires knowing how to navigate a grocery store, healthy tech use requires **digital literacy** - the ability to choose and use tools in ways that serve our long-term well-being.

Digital literacy programs, especially for older adults and marginalized groups, can:

- Build confidence in using devices and apps.

- Teach strategies for safe and intentional online interaction.

- Reduce the risk of scams, which can erode trust in online engagement.

Blending the Online and Offline

The most promising uses of technology **bridge** the gap between online and offline life rather than replacing one with the other:

- Event platforms that help people find local meetups.

- Messaging apps that coordinate in-person activities.

- Online communities that organize offline service projects.

When technology is used as a coordination tool rather than a destination in itself, it can amplify rather than dilute real-world connection.

Policy and Regulation

Governments have a role to play in shaping the digital environment:

- **Transparency**: Requiring tech companies to share data on the mental health impacts of their platforms.

- **Safety Standards**: Setting limits on harmful design practices (e.g., infinite scrolling, addictive reward loops).

- **Funding Pro-Connection Platforms**: Supporting public-interest social networks that prioritize quality interaction over advertising revenue.

The Tech Balance Test

If you're wondering whether your own tech use is helping or harming your social life, consider this quick check:

- Do you leave an online interaction feeling more connected or more inadequate?

- Does your online time inspire offline action or replace it?

- Are your most important relationships maintained primarily through a screen?

If your answers lean toward the negative, it might be time to shift your habits toward more intentional, relationship-centered use.

From Tool to Ally

Technology will never replace the warmth of a hug, the comfort of a shared meal, or the energy of a live conversation. But if designed and used well, it can be an ally in building and sustaining those moments. The challenge is not to reject technology, but to **bend it toward connection**.

In Chapter 7, we'll explore the **built environment** - how the design of our cities, neighborhoods, and public spaces can either foster connection or feed isolation. Just as digital architecture matters online, physical architecture matters offline.

Chapter 7 – Our Built Worlds: Designing for Connection

Imagine walking down a lively street: shop doors are propped open, the smell of coffee drifts from a corner café, kids laugh in a nearby park, and a neighbor waves from their stoop. Now picture a different scene: six-lane traffic roaring past strip malls, empty sidewalks baking in the sun, and homes spaced so far apart you barely know who lives next door.

Both are examples of the **built environment** - the human-made surroundings where we live, work, and play. And both shape how often, and how easily, we connect with other people.

While loneliness is often framed as an emotional or social issue, it's also **a spatial issue**. Our streets, buildings, public spaces, and transportation systems all act as either bridges or barriers to connection.

The Physical Architecture of Loneliness

Humans evolved in environments where connection was built into survival - small groups, shared shelters, and collective gathering around food and fire. In contrast, many modern cities are designed for efficiency, not interaction.

Common features of **disconnection-oriented design** include:

- **Car dominance**: Wide roads and sprawling suburbs make walking unpleasant or unsafe, reducing casual encounters.

- **Single-use zoning**: Separating homes from shops and workplaces forces long commutes, leaving less time for socializing.

- **Lack of public spaces**: Few parks, plazas, or community centers means fewer opportunities to meet casually.

- **Privatized amenities**: Social spaces that require payment or membership exclude low-income residents.

These design choices aren't just inconvenient - they can actively erode social capital, the network of relationships that sustains community trust and cooperation.

The Power of "Third Places"

Sociologist Ray Oldenburg popularized the term **"third places"** - informal gathering spots outside home (the first place) and work (the second place). Examples include cafés, libraries, barber shops, parks, and even certain grocery stores.

Third places are crucial for:

- **Low-stakes interaction**: Chatting with the barista or fellow dog owners at the park.

- **Weak ties**: Acquaintanceships that broaden our social networks and sense of belonging.

- **Community identity**: Places where local culture and traditions can be shared.

Unfortunately, many third places have been disappearing due to rising rents, commercial redevelopment, and shifting leisure habits. Without them, spontaneous interaction becomes rare, and relationships must be scheduled - making them more likely to be postponed or dropped altogether.

Urban Density Done Right

High-density living gets a bad reputation for being impersonal, but density isn't the problem - **design is**. Dense areas that integrate walkable streets, mixed-use buildings, and accessible public transport can create vibrant networks of daily interaction.

Examples of pro-connection urban planning:

- **Transit-based urbanism**: Clustering homes, shops, and community spaces around transit hubs.

- **Mixed-use zoning**: Allowing residential, commercial, and recreational spaces to coexist within walkable distances.

- **Pedestrian-first design**: Wide sidewalks, traffic calming measures, and street furniture encourage people to linger.

- **Pocket parks and micro-plazas**: Small but frequent gathering spaces within neighborhoods.

Contrast this with "bedroom communities," where residents commute long distances to work, spend minimal time in their neighborhoods, and have limited options for casual interaction.

Rural Isolation: A Different Geography of Disconnection

While urban design challenges get much attention, rural areas face their own set of barriers:

- Long distances between homes and services.

- Limited public transportation.

- Fewer public gathering spaces.

- Outmigration of younger residents, leaving behind smaller, aging populations.

49

For rural communities, **transportation and mobility solutions** are as important as physical gathering spaces. Without them, even a well-designed community center or park can remain inaccessible to those who most need it.

Transportation as a Social Connector

Public transport is often discussed in terms of climate impact or economic efficiency, but it's also a **social infrastructure**. A well-designed transit system:

- Brings people into shared spaces.
- Makes it easier for low-income residents to access events and amenities.
- Encourages the chance encounters that spark connection.

Conversely, poor or unsafe transportation options can trap people at home, intensifying isolation - especially among older adults, people with disabilities, and those without cars.

Designing for All Ages

Environments that foster connection must be accessible across life stages and abilities:

- **Child-friendly**: Playgrounds near seating areas encourage intergenerational mingling.
- **Youth-oriented**: Safe, informal hangout spots can reduce risky behaviors and support identity formation.
- **Age-friendly**: Benches, shade, ramps, and well-lit paths make public spaces usable for older adults.

Intergenerational design, such as **combined daycare and senior centers** in Japan, creates opportunities for different age groups to interact daily - strengthening community bonds and mutual understanding.

Safety, Perception, and Belonging

A public space can only foster connection if people feel safe using it. That means addressing:

- **Physical safety**: Well-lit streets, maintained pathways, visible signage.

- **Social safety**: Reducing harassment, discrimination, and exclusionary practices in public areas.

- **Cultural belonging**: Designing spaces that reflect and respect the diversity of the community.

Examples of Connection-Driven Design

- **The Dutch "Chat Checkout"**: Grocery store lanes for customers who want conversation, not speed.

- **London's Play Streets**: Temporary street closures that let neighbors gather, children play, and local musicians perform.

- **Bogotá's Ciclovía**: Weekly citywide event where major roads are closed to cars and opened for walking, cycling, and dancing.

- **Singapore's void decks**: Open communal spaces on the ground floor of public housing, used for everything from weddings to game nights.

From Concrete to Community

The design of our environments sends a message about what - and who - we value. Cities and towns that prioritize wide highways over walkable streets, or luxury developments over community centers, signal that efficiency and profit outweigh connection and belonging.

But when urban planning centers human interaction, the benefits extend far beyond reducing loneliness:

- **Economic**: Stronger local businesses through increased foot traffic.

- **Health**: More walking, more green space, less stress.

- **Resilience**: Communities that know each other are better able to respond to crises.

Policy Levers for Change

Local governments can embed connection into the DNA of city planning by:

- Mandating community space in new developments.

- Offering tax incentives for businesses that serve as informal gathering spots.

- Funding public events in parks and plazas.

- Integrating loneliness metrics into urban development assessments.

Design Is Destiny

The built world doesn't just shape how we move - it shapes how we relate to one another. If we want to reverse the loneliness epidemic, we must treat **connection as a design principle**, not an accidental byproduct.

In **Chapter 8**, we'll leave the streets and step inside the human body again - exploring the **molecular mechanisms** that explain why loneliness is so damaging to our health, and how social connection quite literally gets under our skin.

54

Chapter 8 – The Body on Alert: How Loneliness Rewrites Our Health at the Molecular Level

When we think about loneliness, we usually picture feelings - an ache in the chest, a sense of emptiness, maybe a restless night staring at the ceiling. But science tells us that loneliness is not just a mood - it's a **biological event**. It can change the way our bodies function, right down to the level of genes and immune cells.

In recent years, researchers have discovered something remarkable: the human body treats prolonged loneliness almost like it treats physical danger. To our ancient wiring, being alone meant being vulnerable - cut off from the group's protection against predators, accidents, or starvation. Our biology responds as if danger is imminent, even if we're just sitting safely at home with a smartphone in hand.

Loneliness as a Survival Signal

Imagine you're a hunter-gatherer thousands of years ago. One morning you find yourself separated from your group. You're more likely to be injured, attacked, or miss out on food. Your body needs to be ready for trouble.

Evolution built in a **biological alarm system**:

- **Ramp up inflammation** to heal wounds quickly if injured.

- **Dial down antiviral responses** because infection risk from others is lower when alone.

That system made perfect sense in the wild. But in modern life, loneliness can persist for months or years - and the "always-on" survival mode becomes toxic.

The Inflammation Problem

Inflammation is the immune system's way of responding to threats. In short bursts, it's lifesaving - fighting off infection, helping wounds heal. But chronic, low-grade inflammation is a different story. It quietly fuels conditions like:

- Atherosclerosis (hardening of the arteries)
- Type 2 diabetes
- Alzheimer's disease
- Certain cancers

Lonely individuals show elevated markers of inflammation, such as **C-reactive protein (CRP)** and **interleukin-6 (IL-6)**. Over time, this constant "molecular fire" damages tissues, disrupts normal cell function, and accelerates aging.

A Weakened Antiviral Defense

The flip side of the inflammatory surge is a **suppressed antiviral response**. Studies have found that people experiencing chronic loneliness have lower activity in **type I interferon** genes, which are critical for fighting off viruses.

This means lonely individuals aren't just more likely to catch infections - they often take longer to recover. During flu season, or in the face of new viruses, that vulnerability has obvious consequences.

Stress Hormones in Overdrive

Loneliness also activates the body's stress-response system, particularly the **hypothalamic–pituitary–adrenal (HPA) axis**. This system releases cortisol, a hormone that helps us deal with immediate challenges. But with prolonged activation:

- Cortisol rhythms become dysregulated.

- Blood pressure stays elevated.

- Sleep quality declines.

Over time, this constant state of alert contributes to cardiovascular disease, metabolic problems, and impaired immune function.

The Brain's Pain Response

One of the most striking findings in loneliness research is that **social pain and physical pain share neural pathways**. Brain scans show that when people feel socially excluded, areas like the **dorsal anterior cingulate cortex** and **anterior insula** light up - the same regions activated by physical injury.

This overlap explains why we use phrases like "hurt feelings" or "broken heart" - the brain isn't speaking metaphorically; it's experiencing the pain as real. In one study, even a dose of acetaminophen (Tylenol) reduced not only reports of social hurt but also the brain activity associated with it.

Sleep Disruption: The Quiet Saboteur

Lonely people often report restless or fragmented sleep. It's not just that they stay up late scrolling their phones - loneliness can actually keep the brain on high alert, scanning for threats even during rest.

Poor sleep has a cascade effect:

- Weakened immune response.

- Higher inflammation.

- Reduced cognitive performance.

- Lower emotional regulation, which makes social interaction harder.

It's a vicious loop: loneliness disrupts sleep, and poor sleep makes loneliness worse.

The Cognitive Toll

Prolonged loneliness affects not just mood but **cognitive function**:

- Faster decline in memory, attention, and processing speed in older adults.

- Increased risk of developing dementia - by as much as **50%**.

- Possible "prodromal" role, meaning loneliness might signal early brain changes before other symptoms appear.

The exact mechanisms are still being studied, but scientists suspect that reduced social engagement deprives the brain of stimulation, while inflammation and stress hormones accelerate neurodegeneration.

Behavioral Pathways: How Biology Shapes Habits

The physiological effects of loneliness often influence behavior in ways that reinforce the problem:

- **Fatigue and low motivation** make socializing harder.

- **Heightened threat sensitivity** leads to misinterpreting neutral interactions as negative.

- **Self-protection** instincts push people to withdraw further, avoiding perceived risks.

This creates a self-perpetuating cycle: the body's defense systems, meant to protect, end up trapping the person in deeper isolation.

Loneliness Across the Lifespan: Different Biology, Same Risk

The biological consequences of loneliness appear in every age group, but the triggers and patterns differ:

- **Adolescents**: Hormonal changes and developing brain regions make them more sensitive to social exclusion.

- **Adults**: Chronic work stress and caregiving responsibilities can combine with loneliness to increase cardiovascular risk.

- **Older adults**: Immune aging (immunosenescence) and pre-existing conditions make the inflammatory effects of loneliness especially dangerous.

Reversing the Damage

The science is clear: the biology of loneliness is not irreversible. Social reconnection can calm the body's overactive alarm systems and restore healthier immune function. Interventions that show promise include:

- **Group-based activities**: Combining physical movement with social interaction (e.g., walking clubs) improves both inflammation markers and mood.

- **Cognitive-behavioral therapy**: Reduces the threat sensitivity that fuels biological stress.

- **Mindfulness and meditation**: Lower cortisol levels and inflammation.

- **Consistent sleep routines**: Help restore normal stress hormone cycles.

Even small, positive interactions - chatting with a neighbor, volunteering, attending a class - can start to shift both the psychological and biological patterns of loneliness.

Why This Matters for Public Health

When policymakers hear about loneliness, they might picture sadness or low mood - not inflammatory cytokines or gene expression changes. But understanding the **molecular footprint** of loneliness reframes it as a legitimate medical priority, one that intersects with cardiovascular health, dementia prevention, and even pandemic preparedness.

If loneliness can influence our bodies at the cellular level, then social connection isn't just "nice to have" - it's as essential as nutrition and exercise.

In Chapter 9, we'll shift from biology back to psychology, exploring **how loneliness alters the mind's outlook, decision-making, and capacity for trust** - and why breaking its mental loops can be just as important as addressing its physical effects.

Chapter 9 – The Mind in Retreat: How Loneliness Shapes Thinking and Emotion

When you're lonely, it's not just your heart that aches or your immune system that struggles. Loneliness can get inside your head - altering how you think, how you interpret the world, and even how you remember events. Over time, these mental shifts can trap you in a self-reinforcing loop, making it harder to reconnect even when opportunities arise.

In this chapter, we'll explore how loneliness affects the mind - its emotional toll, its cognitive impacts, and the subtle but powerful ways it changes the lens through which we see the world.

The Emotional Weight of Loneliness

Loneliness is closely linked to a range of mental health challenges, particularly **depression and anxiety**. This is partly because loneliness and these conditions share common symptoms:

- Loss of motivation.

- Low self-worth.

- Heightened negative thinking.

The relationship is **bidirectional**:

- Depression can lead to social withdrawal, which reduces connection.

- Reduced connection deepens loneliness, which worsens depression.

It's a cycle that's especially hard to break because loneliness saps the very energy needed to take social risks.

Anxiety and the Hypervigilant Mind

When you feel lonely for a long time, the brain's social threat radar becomes hypersensitive. This hypervigilance evolved to protect us - if you're isolated in the wild, you need to be extra alert to danger. But in modern social life, it often backfires.

Lonely individuals are more likely to:

- Interpret ambiguous social cues as negative ("They didn't text back - maybe they don't like me").

- Remember negative interactions more vividly than positive ones.

- Assume rejection before it happens, leading to self-protective withdrawal.

This "better safe than sorry" approach may shield against occasional hurt, but it also shuts down the opportunities for connection that could resolve the loneliness.

The Cognitive Load of Disconnection

Loneliness doesn't just change *what* you think - it changes *how well* you think. Studies show that chronic loneliness is associated with:

- Reduced **executive function** (planning, problem-solving, impulse control).

- Slower **processing speed**.

- Weaker **working memory**.

Part of this may be due to the stress and sleep disruption loneliness causes, but it also relates to the loss of cognitive stimulation. Social interaction challenges the brain - remembering names, interpreting facial expressions, adapting to conversational shifts. Without regular "mental workouts" through social engagement, these skills can dull.

The Dementia Link

For older adults, loneliness is a significant risk factor for dementia, increasing the likelihood by as much as **50%**. Researchers suggest several possible pathways:

- **Biological**: Chronic inflammation and stress hormones accelerate neurodegeneration.

- **Behavioral**: Loneliness often reduces physical activity and healthy habits, both of which protect brain health.

- **Cognitive**: Lack of social stimulation weakens neural pathways involved in memory and reasoning.

While not all lonely older adults develop dementia, the risk is serious enough that reducing social isolation is increasingly seen as a **dementia prevention strategy**.

Memory and Mood: A Dangerous Combination

Loneliness tends to bias memory toward the negative. When socially disconnected, people recall rejection and failure more clearly than acceptance and success. This has two effects:

1. **Mood reinforcement**: Negative memories deepen feelings of sadness and pessimism.

2. **Expectation shaping**: Past perceived failures color expectations for future interactions.

In other words, your brain starts to curate a highlight reel of the worst moments - and then predicts more of the same.

The Role of Self-Fulfilling Prophecies

When negative expectations take root, they can change behavior in ways that make those expectations come true. For example:

- Expecting to be ignored may make you less friendly, causing others to actually ignore you.

- Assuming you won't be invited may lead you to avoid events entirely, ensuring you stay isolated.

These self-fulfilling prophecies are a hallmark of chronic loneliness and a major reason it's so resistant to change without intentional intervention.

Psychological Safety and Trust

Trust is the foundation of social connection, but loneliness erodes it. Lonely people often report lower trust in others, partly because repeated feelings of exclusion create an internal narrative that "people let me down."

The result is a **shrinking social risk tolerance** - an unwillingness to engage with new people or deepen existing relationships. Without trust, relationships struggle to grow beyond surface-level acquaintance.

Breaking the Mental Loops

The good news is that the psychological patterns of loneliness can be interrupted. Evidence-based strategies include:

Cognitive-Behavioral Therapy (CBT)

CBT helps people identify and challenge negative social beliefs, such as "Nobody wants to talk to me" or "I'm boring." Over time, replacing these with more balanced thoughts can reduce social anxiety and encourage re-engagement.

Behavioral Activation

Instead of waiting to feel ready to socialize, this approach encourages people to start with small, manageable actions - like saying hello to a neighbor or attending a short community event. These small successes build confidence and counteract negative expectations.

Mindfulness Practices

Mindfulness reduces rumination on past social hurts and helps people respond to interactions as they are, rather than through the filter of past rejection. This can lower emotional reactivity and open the door to more positive exchanges.

Gratitude and Positive Recall

Keeping a journal of small positive interactions - even something as simple as a smile from a stranger - can counter the brain's negativity bias. Over time, this rewires memory to include more positive social moments.

The Role of Community in Mental Recovery

While individual therapies can be powerful, recovery is faster and more sustainable when supported by **community-based interventions**. Group activities - whether hobby clubs, volunteering, or group exercise - provide both the mental stimulation and the emotional reinforcement needed to reframe loneliness.

These settings also offer opportunities to **practice** social skills in low-pressure environments, reinforcing the cognitive and emotional benefits over time.

Why Addressing the Mind Matters for the Body

The mental loops of loneliness aren't just a psychological issue - they directly influence physical health. A hypervigilant mind keeps the body's stress systems activated, reinforcing inflammation, poor sleep, and weakened immunity. Conversely, a calmer, more trusting mindset helps the body stand down from its constant state of alert.

From Retreat to Reach

The journey out of loneliness often starts in the mind - challenging the stories we tell ourselves about who we are and how others see us. When those stories shift, behavior shifts too, creating new opportunities for connection.

In Chapter 10, we'll step back and look at loneliness from a broader perspective - examining **how it became recognized as a public health crisis** and why health agencies now treat it as seriously as smoking or obesity.

Chapter 10 – From Social Pain to Public Health: Why Loneliness Demands Urgent Action

For most of history, loneliness was treated as a private matter - a melancholy mood, a phase to be endured, or, at worst, a personal failing. You might talk about it with a close friend or write about it in a diary, but it was rarely something you'd expect to see on the agenda of the World Health Organization.

Today, that has changed. Loneliness has stepped out of the shadows and into the policy spotlight. Health agencies now discuss it alongside smoking, obesity, and physical inactivity as a major public health threat. In 2025, the World Health Assembly passed its first-ever resolution on **social connection as a global health priority**, a landmark acknowledgment that disconnection is not just a personal sadness - it's a societal risk factor.

In this chapter, we'll explore how loneliness made the leap from emotional state to public health crisis, why it's now being compared to chronic disease risk factors, and what this shift means for the future of health policy.

The Epidemiology of Loneliness

Public health agencies now talk about loneliness using the language of epidemiology - the same way they discuss heart disease or infectious outbreaks.

Prevalence:

- Globally, about **1 in 6 people** experience loneliness at any given time.

- In the United States, surveys suggest around **50% of adults** report loneliness at least some of the time.

- In the European Union, **13%** report feeling lonely most or all of the time, with much higher rates in certain demographics.

These numbers alone warrant attention - but the true public health urgency comes from the consequences.

The Risk Profile: Comparable to Smoking or Obesity

The health effects of chronic loneliness are stark and well-documented:

- **29% increased risk** of premature death for socially isolated individuals.

- **26% increased risk** for lonely individuals specifically.

- Elevated risks for heart disease, stroke, dementia, depression, and suicide.

When then–U.S. Surgeon General Dr. Vivek Murthy declared in 2023 that the health impact of loneliness was equivalent to smoking **15 cigarettes a day**, it was a turning point in public awareness. The metaphor cut through the assumption that loneliness was "just feelings" and put it in the same category as lifestyle-related disease risks.

The Social-Ecological Model: Why This Is a System Problem

One reason loneliness is now a public health priority is that it fits squarely within the **social-ecological model** - a framework that looks at health through multiple levels of influence:

1. **Individual** – Mental health, social skills, cognitive biases.

2. **Interpersonal** – Relationships, family dynamics, peer networks.

3. **Community** – Neighborhood design, local institutions, workplace culture.

4. **Societal** – Economic policy, digital regulation, cultural norms.

Public health professionals see that no single intervention will work without addressing all these layers simultaneously.

Why Public Health Agencies Are Getting Involved Now

Several factors have converged to push loneliness into the global health agenda:

1. Mounting Scientific Evidence

Over the past two decades, research has quantified the link between social disconnection and physical health outcomes. Large-scale meta-analyses, like those by Dr. Julianne Holt-Lunstad, have shown that the mortality risk of loneliness rivals that of other well-established health hazards.

2. The COVID-19 Pandemic

The pandemic acted as a natural experiment in mass isolation. Lockdowns and distancing measures dramatically reduced in-person social contact for billions, and the aftereffects linger - especially for those who lost loved ones, missed developmental milestones, or never fully reestablished their social networks.

3. Policy Precedents

Countries like the UK and Japan have already appointed government ministers or agencies dedicated to loneliness, demonstrating that it can be addressed at the policy level. These examples have encouraged other nations to follow suit.

4. Economic Impact

Loneliness costs money. It's linked to higher healthcare use, lower productivity, and greater workplace turnover. The U.S. health system alone may spend billions annually treating conditions exacerbated by social disconnection.

Case Studies: Policy in Action

United Kingdom

In 2018, the UK appointed a **Minister for Loneliness** and rolled out a cross-government strategy that included:

- A national loneliness measurement framework.
- Social prescribing programs linking patients to community groups.
- Public awareness campaigns to reduce stigma.

Japan

Facing rising numbers of socially withdrawn individuals (*hikikomori*), Japan appointed a **Minister of Loneliness** in 2021. Initiatives include:

- Funding for community centers.
- Outreach to isolated older adults.
- Support programs for reclusive youth.

United States

The 2023 Surgeon General's **National Strategy to Advance Social Connection** outlined six pillars, from strengthening social infrastructure to reforming digital environments. This marks one of the most comprehensive government-level responses in the world.

Challenges in Public Health Implementation

Recognizing loneliness as a public health issue is one thing; addressing it is another. Key challenges include:

- **Measurement:** How do you track something subjective? Tools like the UCLA Loneliness Scale and single-item measures are now being used in surveys, but standardization is still in progress.

- **Stigma:** Many people still see loneliness as a personal weakness, making them reluctant to report it.

- **Equity:** Marginalized groups face unique barriers to connection, so interventions must be culturally and contextually tailored.

- **Sustainability:** Short-term interventions often fade without systemic change - urban planning, workplace policy, and community investment are long-term necessities.

From Awareness to Action: The Role of Public Health Campaigns

Public health agencies have decades of experience changing behaviors through campaigns - seatbelt use, smoking cessation, vaccination. Loneliness campaigns borrow similar strategies:

- **Normalize the conversation** ("Everyone feels lonely sometimes").

- **Provide concrete actions** ("Join a local group," "Call an old friend," "Check in on a neighbor").

- **Highlight benefits** of connection for physical health, not just emotional well-being.

Some campaigns now frame connection as a **health habit**, akin to daily exercise.

Why This Shift Matters

Framing loneliness as a public health crisis changes the conversation in three important ways:

1. **Legitimacy** – People take it seriously, reducing stigma.
2. **Funding** – It opens the door to government budgets and research grants.
3. **Accountability** – Governments, employers, and institutions become responsible for fostering social health.

The Next Steps in the Global Health Movement

As the WHO resolution moves into implementation, watch for:

- National "connection strategies" modeled on the UK and U.S. examples.

- Integration of loneliness metrics into health surveillance systems.

- Cross-sector collaborations - urban planners, tech companies, educators - working toward shared goals.

- More rigorous evaluation of intervention effectiveness over time.

Loneliness as a Social Determinant of Health

Public health increasingly recognizes **social connection as a determinant of health** - on par with housing, education, and income. This perspective doesn't just aim to treat the symptoms of loneliness; it seeks to build the social infrastructure that prevents it in the first place.

In Chapter 11, we'll return to the personal level - exploring practical ways individuals can reclaim connection in their own lives, while acknowledging the systemic challenges they may face. This will be the bridge from policy to personal action.

Chapter 11 – Reclaiming Connection: Practical Steps for a More Connected Life

By now, we've explored loneliness from almost every angle - its history, cultural drivers, biological effects, and recognition as a public health crisis. But while governments, workplaces, and communities all have a role to play, change often starts with individual action.

That doesn't mean the responsibility for fixing loneliness rests solely on your shoulders. Systemic problems require systemic solutions. But there's power in small, intentional steps. In fact, research suggests that even modest increases in daily social contact can significantly improve mood, health, and life satisfaction.

This chapter is about reclaiming that power - not through grand gestures or instant makeovers, but through realistic, sustainable habits that help rebuild your personal web of connection.

Step 1: Redefine What Connection Means for You

One of the biggest myths about loneliness is that it's simply a matter of "not knowing enough people." In reality, the quality of connections matters far more than the quantity.

Take a moment to reflect:

- What kinds of interactions make you feel most alive?

- Who in your life leaves you feeling energized rather than drained?

- Which environments make you feel like you belong?

Your answers will help you focus your energy where it matters. For some, that might mean deepening existing friendships; for others, it's about finding spaces where you can meet like-minded people.

Step 2: Start Small, Start Local

When loneliness has been around for a while, the idea of diving into large social events can feel overwhelming. The key is to start with **low-pressure, low-stakes interactions**:

- Chat with a neighbor while checking the mail.
- Ask the barista how their day is going.
- Say hello to the person walking their dog on your street.

These micro-interactions might seem trivial, but they create a subtle shift in your social landscape. Psychologists call this building **"weak ties"** - casual connections that add up to a broader sense of belonging over time.

Step 3: Use Technology Intentionally

As we saw in Chapter 6, technology can either bridge or widen the connection gap. The trick is to use it **as a tool for offline connection** rather than a substitute for it:

- Join online groups with the goal of meeting in person (book clubs, hobby meetups).
- Use messaging apps to set up phone calls or walks.
- Limit passive scrolling in favor of active engagement - sending direct messages or commenting thoughtfully.

When you catch yourself endlessly scrolling, ask: *Is this making me feel more connected or more disconnected?*

Step 4: Revisit Old Connections

Sometimes the fastest way to strengthen your social network is to repair or rekindle existing ties. Reach out to:

- Old friends you've lost touch with.

- Former coworkers you enjoyed spending time with.

- Relatives you only see at holidays.

It doesn't have to be a big production. A short message like, "I was thinking about you the other day - how have you been?" can open the door.

Step 5: Volunteer Your Time and Skills

Volunteering is one of the most effective ways to meet people while building purpose into your life. It works for several reasons:

- Shared activity gives you something to talk about right away.

- Helping others boosts mood and self-esteem.

- Many volunteer groups meet regularly, providing consistent contact.

From mentoring students to helping at a food bank, there's likely a cause in your area that could use your talents.

Step 6: Prioritize Group-Based Activities

Group activities combine two key ingredients for connection - **shared purpose** and **repeated interaction**. Examples include:

- Community sports leagues.
- Choirs or music groups.
- Cooking or language classes.
- Walking clubs.

Repeated contact builds familiarity, and familiarity builds trust. The first meeting might feel awkward; the fifth will feel more natural.

Step 7: Learn the Art of Invitation

Many people wait to be invited, but becoming the inviter can change everything. Start small:

- Invite a coworker for coffee.
- Suggest a movie night with a friend.
- Organize a casual potluck.

You might be surprised by how many people are eager for connection but hesitant to make the first move.

Step 8: Build Connection Into Your Routine

Connection becomes easier when it's woven into daily life. Some ideas:

- Walk at the same time each day in your neighborhood to see familiar faces.

- Go to the same café or library regularly.

- Schedule weekly check-in calls with friends or family.

Habits remove the need for constant decision-making - and social habits are no different.

Step 9: Address the Psychological Barriers

Loneliness can create mental loops that hold us back, as we saw in Chapter 9. Consider:

- **Therapy** (especially cognitive-behavioral therapy) to challenge negative assumptions about social interactions.

- **Mindfulness** to stay present during conversations rather than ruminating on past hurts.

- **Self-compassion practices** to reduce the self-criticism that often accompanies loneliness.

When your mind is less focused on threat detection, it's easier to notice and engage with opportunities for connection.

Step 10: Recognize That Setbacks Are Normal

Not every social interaction will go perfectly - and that's okay. Even the most socially confident people have awkward moments or experience rejection. The difference is, they keep trying.

Think of social connection like physical fitness: you wouldn't quit going to the gym because one workout felt off. Similarly, keep showing up for connection, even if some attempts fall flat.

A Note on Special Circumstances

Some situations require tailored strategies:

- **Chronic illness or disability**: Seek support groups - both online and in-person - that understand your specific challenges.

- **New parenthood**: Join parenting groups or "baby and me" classes for both adult company and peer advice.

- **Relocation**: Look for local newcomer events or expat communities.

- **Grief**: Bereavement groups provide understanding peers when friends or family struggle to know what to say.

Why Personal Effort Still Matters in a Systemic Problem

It's true - structural factors like urban design, work culture, and inequality make connection harder for many people. But small, personal actions are still a critical piece of the puzzle. They create ripple effects:

- Strengthening your own resilience.

- Making your corner of the community warmer.

- Modeling connection habits for others.

And when enough individuals start weaving more connection into daily life, it shifts the broader culture too.

From Effort to Ease

The first steps may feel awkward or tiring - especially if loneliness has been your companion for a while. But over time, something remarkable happens: connection starts to feel natural again. Your brain stops scanning for rejection. Social interactions become energizing rather than draining.

This is the moment when loneliness loosens its grip - not because life is perfect, but because you've rebuilt the bridges that let warmth, trust, and belonging flow back in.

In Chapter 12, we'll zoom back out and look at **workplaces as connection engines** - and how they can either be powerful antidotes to loneliness or major contributors to it. Since so many of us spend a third of our lives at work, this is a critical arena for change.

Chapter 12 – Communities at Work: How Workplaces Can Foster Connection

For many adults, the workplace is the single biggest arena for daily social contact. We spend roughly one-third of our lives working - and for better or worse, that environment shapes our sense of belonging. A supportive workplace can feel like a second home, filled with camaraderie, shared purpose, and mutual care. But a disconnected workplace can be isolating, competitive, and draining, leaving employees lonelier than if they'd stayed home.

In recent years, loneliness in the workplace has emerged as both a **mental health crisis** and a **business problem**. It's linked to burnout, turnover, and reduced productivity - costing organizations billions annually in lost potential. But here's the hopeful side: because work is such a central part of modern life, it's also a powerful place to build and strengthen social bonds.

The New Shape of Workplace Loneliness

Workplace loneliness isn't simply about whether people like their coworkers. It's more complex, shaped by:

- **Structural changes**: The rise of remote and hybrid work, automation, and gig economy jobs has reduced casual in-person contact.

- **Cultural norms**: An emphasis on competition, efficiency, and "always-on" productivity can sideline social connection.

- **Organizational design**: Physical layout, team structures, and leadership styles all influence how often - and how well - people interact.

The Remote Work Paradox

Remote and hybrid work have obvious advantages - flexibility, reduced commute times, and greater access for people with disabilities or caregiving responsibilities. But they also come with **connection challenges**:

- Fewer "water cooler" moments for spontaneous conversation.
- Social interactions becoming scheduled, agenda-driven meetings.
- A reliance on digital communication, which lacks nonverbal cues and can feel transactional.

Some remote workers report feeling **geographically unmoored**, with professional ties that are functional but emotionally thin.

The Cost of Disconnection at Work

Workplace loneliness has measurable impacts on both individuals and organizations:

- **Reduced performance**: Lonely workers are less engaged and more likely to disengage from collaborative tasks.
- **Burnout risk**: Without supportive colleagues, stress has fewer outlets and recovery periods are shorter.
- **Higher turnover**: Employees who feel disconnected are more likely to leave, especially in tight labor markets.
- **Innovation loss**: Creativity thrives in environments of trust and open dialogue - two things loneliness undermines.

The ripple effects extend beyond the office walls: workplace loneliness can spill over into home life, affecting relationships, mood, and even physical health.

The Anatomy of a Connected Workplace

So what does a pro-connection workplace look like? It's not just about friendly coworkers or occasional parties. The most effective workplaces build connection into the **core of their operations**, combining physical, cultural, and procedural strategies.

1. Leadership That Models Connection

Leaders set the tone. When managers:

- Regularly check in on team members as people, not just employees,

- Share vulnerabilities and personal stories,

- Encourage collaboration over competition,
  they normalize connection as part of the job.

2. Physical Spaces That Invite Interaction

Office design matters:

- Open collaboration areas balanced with private spaces for focus.

- Kitchens, lounges, and communal tables where people can gather informally.

- Visual cues like bulletin boards for community announcements and celebrations.

Even in remote setups, "digital office spaces" (persistent chat rooms, informal video hangouts) can mimic these communal areas.

3. Rituals and Rhythms

Rituals create predictability and shared experience. Examples:

- Weekly team check-ins that include personal highs and lows.
- Monthly "learning lunches" or cross-department socials.
- Celebrating milestones - birthdays, project completions, work anniversaries.

These regular touchpoints keep connection from being an afterthought.

4. Opportunities for Cross-Team Collaboration

When departments operate in silos, relationships shrink to immediate coworkers. Encouraging cross-functional projects and shared problem-solving broadens networks and creates more chances for trust to grow.

5. Support for Life Beyond Work

Workplaces that acknowledge employees' whole lives - not just their professional output - tend to see stronger connections. This might include:

- Flexible hours for caregiving responsibilities.
- Mental health days and wellness programs.
- Resource groups for parents, veterans, LGBTQ+ employees, and others.

Remote and Hybrid Connection Strategies

For distributed teams, connection needs deliberate architecture:

- **Virtual coffee chats**: Randomly pair employees for 15-minute informal calls.

- **Collaborative rituals**: Start meetings with a light check-in question ("What's one small win from your week?").

- **Shared digital spaces**: Slack or Teams channels for non-work interests - pets, hobbies, recipes.

- **Annual or semi-annual retreats**: In-person gatherings to strengthen bonds that digital tools can't fully replicate.

The Role of Psychological Safety

No matter how many social events a workplace offers, employees won't connect deeply without **psychological safety** - the belief that they can speak up, make mistakes, and be themselves without fear of humiliation or punishment. Psychological safety is linked to:

- Higher trust.

- More collaboration.

- Better problem-solving.

Loneliness often thrives where psychological safety is low, because employees feel guarded and reluctant to share authentically.

The Business Case for Connection

While some leaders still see connection as "soft" or optional, the data say otherwise. Studies have shown that companies with high employee engagement:

- See **21% higher profitability**.

- Have **41% lower absenteeism**.

- Experience greater customer satisfaction.

Connection is not just about employee happiness - it's a driver of performance.

Social Prescribing in the Workplace

Borrowing from public health, some organizations are experimenting with **social prescribing** - linking employees to resources or groups that foster connection, both inside and outside work. For example:

- Funding hobby clubs.

- Partnering with local gyms or arts organizations.

- Offering stipends for classes or community events.

Pitfalls to Avoid

Efforts to boost connection can backfire if they:

- **Feel forced**: Mandatory fun can make employees resentful.

- **Ignore workload**: Scheduling events without adjusting deadlines adds stress.

- **Exclude some employees**: Activities that assume physical ability, extroversion, or certain cultural norms can alienate rather than unite.

A Shared Responsibility

Building a connected workplace isn't solely HR's job. It's a shared responsibility:

- Leaders create the vision and allocate resources.

- Managers model and reinforce connection behaviors.

- Employees engage actively and look out for one another.

When everyone participates, connection becomes a living part of the organizational culture, not just an initiative.

From Colleagues to Community

At their best, workplaces can become communities - places where people not only earn a living but also find meaning, growth, and friendship. In such environments, workdays leave people more connected, not more depleted.

In Chapter 13, we'll widen the lens again - looking at how **governments are stepping in** to create policies and initiatives that foster social connection across entire populations, from city design to national campaigns.

90

Chapter 13 – Governments Step In: Policy as a Tool for Connection

When most people think of government policy, they picture budgets, taxes, or infrastructure - not friendship, conversation, and belonging. But in recent years, a surprising shift has occurred: governments are treating loneliness not just as a personal or cultural issue, but as a measurable public health and economic concern that can - and should - be addressed through legislation and planning.

From national loneliness strategies to citywide urban design initiatives, policymakers are starting to recognize what researchers have been saying for decades: **social connection is a form of public infrastructure**. Like clean water or electricity, it requires investment, maintenance, and regulation.

The First Movers: UK and Japan

The United Kingdom

The UK was the first country to formally embed loneliness into its policy agenda.

- **2018**: Prime Minister Theresa May appointed the world's first **Minister for Loneliness**.

- Developed a **cross-government strategy** with 60+ commitments spanning health, education, transport, and housing.

- Launched national awareness campaigns to reduce stigma and normalize talking about loneliness.

- Integrated "social prescribing" into the National Health Service (NHS), enabling doctors to refer patients to community activities instead of - or alongside - medical treatments.

Japan

Japan's policies emerged from a specific crisis: the rise of **hikikomori** (acute social withdrawal), especially among young men, and increasing isolation among older adults.

- **2021**: Established a **Minister of Loneliness** to coordinate government and NGO efforts.

- Increased funding for community spaces and outreach programs.

- Supported initiatives like intergenerational housing to combat both youth and elderly isolation.

- Partnered with local governments to identify and assist socially withdrawn individuals.

The United States Steps Up

In 2023, U.S. Surgeon General Dr. Vivek Murthy released the **National Strategy to Advance Social Connection**, the first comprehensive federal plan on loneliness.

The strategy outlined **six pillars**:

1. **Strengthen social infrastructure** – invest in parks, libraries, and community centers.

2. **Enact pro-connection public policies** – e.g., flexible work laws, urban design standards.

3. **Reform digital environments** – promote healthier online spaces.

4. **Deepen community-based programs** – expand volunteer opportunities and civic engagement.

5. **Build a culture of connection** – public campaigns and education.

6. **Track progress** – integrate loneliness metrics into federal health surveys.

The WHO's Global Declaration

In 2025, the **World Health Assembly** passed a resolution declaring social connection a global health priority - putting it on the same level as mental health, tobacco control, and nutrition. This was a pivotal moment for reframing loneliness as:

- A **social determinant of health**.

- A measurable factor in disease prevention.

- A target for cross-sector policy, from transportation to technology.

Policy Tools That Work

Urban and Community Planning

- **Zoning for mixed-use neighborhoods**: Reduces travel distances and fosters casual encounters.

- **Public space investment**: Parks, plazas, and "third places" as core infrastructure.

- **Walkability standards**: Safe sidewalks, lighting, and benches for all ages.

Social Prescribing

- Health professionals "prescribe" participation in community activities like gardening clubs, choirs, or exercise groups.

- UK data suggests that social prescribing can reduce primary care visits and improve self-reported well-being.

Digital Regulation

- Addressing algorithmic designs that promote divisive or addictive content.

- Encouraging platforms to facilitate local, interest-based groups that can meet offline.

- Mandating transparency in platform impact reporting on mental health and social connection.

Education Policy

- Embedding **social-emotional learning** into curricula to help children build and maintain healthy relationships.

- Supporting school-community partnerships that connect families beyond the classroom.

Workplace Legislation

- Flexible work laws that balance productivity with time for community engagement.

- Mandating breaks and limits on excessive overtime, particularly in countries with "overwork" cultures.

Measuring Success

Policymakers face a challenge: **How do you measure something as personal as loneliness?**
Current approaches include:

- Nationwide surveys using the **UCLA Loneliness Scale**.

- Proxy indicators: rates of community participation, volunteerism, and social trust.

- Longitudinal studies tracking health outcomes alongside reported connection levels.

Over time, combining subjective self-reports with objective health and social data will give a clearer picture of policy effectiveness.

Equity in Connection Policy

A universal approach won't work because loneliness affects different groups in different ways:

- **Older adults** may need accessible transportation and age-friendly public spaces.

- **Youth** may benefit more from digital literacy programs and safe offline gathering spaces.

- **Immigrant communities** may need multilingual services and culturally familiar activities.

- **People with disabilities** require not just physical accessibility but also inclusive program design.

Effective policy uses **intersectional analysis** to ensure no group is left behind.

Global Collaboration

Loneliness doesn't stop at borders, and neither should solutions. Countries are beginning to share best practices through:

- WHO working groups.
- International summits on healthy aging and community well-being.
- Research collaborations pooling data from multiple nations.

These forums allow governments to adapt policies that have worked elsewhere rather than reinventing the wheel.

Potential Pitfalls

Government involvement isn't automatically a cure. Policies can fall short if they:

- Focus solely on **awareness campaigns** without funding physical infrastructure.
- Fail to address the **root causes** like poverty, housing insecurity, and discrimination.
- Are implemented without **community input**, resulting in programs nobody uses.

Why Government Matters

Individual effort is vital, but there are limits to what people can do when their environment works against them. Governments control the levers that shape social life on a mass scale - urban design, education, health systems, labor laws, and digital regulation. By embedding connection into these systems, they can create the conditions where personal relationships flourish naturally.

In Chapter 14, we'll imagine what it would look like if this vision were fully realized - a **world designed for belonging**, where cities, workplaces, and digital spaces all work in harmony to keep us connected.

Chapter 14 – A World Designed for Belonging: The Future of Connection

Picture stepping out your front door in the morning and feeling instantly part of something bigger than yourself. Your street is alive with the sounds of neighbors greeting one another, children laughing in a nearby play space, and the aroma of fresh bread drifting from a corner bakery where the baker already knows your name. You wave to an elderly neighbor tending to flowers in the community garden, and a friend from down the block invites you to join an evening storytelling circle at the park.

This is not a quaint throwback to a bygone era - it's a possible future, one where society has made **belonging** a central design principle. In such a world, everything from urban planning to technology platforms to healthcare systems is built with the goal of keeping people meaningfully connected.

From Concept to Culture

The research we've explored in earlier chapters makes one thing clear: connection isn't an optional luxury; it's a public health necessity. But to embed that truth into everyday life, we need more than policies - we need a culture-wide shift.

In a world designed for belonging:

- We'd value **quality of relationships** as much as economic growth.

- Community health indicators would be tracked alongside GDP.

- Cities would be judged not just on traffic flow or housing units, but on the strength of their social fabric.

The Built Environment: Cities That Invite Interaction

The foundation of this future is the **physical landscape**. Our streets, parks, and public buildings would be designed to maximize spontaneous encounters and shared experiences:

- **Mixed-use neighborhoods** ensure homes, shops, schools, and workplaces are within walking distance.

- **Public squares and green spaces** anchor every community, serving as gathering points for events, markets, and casual meet-ups.

- **Safe, shaded walkways** encourage strolling and conversation, not just commuting.

- Housing developments include **common rooms, rooftop gardens, and co-working spaces** where residents can connect.

Urban planners would use "connection audits" to assess how every new project impacts opportunities for social interaction.

Digital Spaces With Human Values

Technology wouldn't disappear in this future - it would evolve. Platforms would be **designed to connect people locally and meaningfully**, not just keep them scrolling.

- Algorithms would prioritize introducing users to nearby events, groups, and volunteering opportunities.

- Digital tools would help maintain **weak ties**, reminding you of acquaintances you haven't seen in a while.

- Social media metrics would focus on **meaningful interactions** rather than likes and follower counts.

In this model, online engagement would consistently lead to offline connection, closing the loop between virtual and physical worlds.

Healthcare as a Hub for Connection

Clinics and hospitals would recognize loneliness as a **social vital sign**. During check-ups, practitioners would ask about your social life alongside questions about diet, exercise, and sleep.

If needed, you could be "prescribed":

- A local walking group.

- An art class at the community center.

- Volunteer opportunities tailored to your skills.

Healthcare systems would partner with civic organizations, making connection-building part of preventive medicine.

Workplaces as Connection Engines

Employment settings would be structured to foster both productivity and belonging:

- Flexible schedules would allow time for community engagement.

- Offices would balance private focus areas with vibrant communal spaces.

- Remote teams would receive regular in-person gatherings, funded and organized as part of the workweek.

- Peer mentorship programs would ensure no employee feels invisible.

Leaders would be trained not only in strategic management but also in **relational leadership** - the skills to create trust, psychological safety, and camaraderie.

Education That Teaches Connection Skills

From early childhood onward, schools would teach **social literacy** - the art and science of building and maintaining healthy relationships. Students would:

- Practice active listening and empathy.
- Learn conflict resolution through role-play.
- Participate in service-learning projects that link them to their broader community.

Graduates wouldn't just be academically ready; they'd be socially fluent.

The Role of Public Rituals and Traditions

In a connected future, communities would create and sustain **shared rituals** - seasonal festivals, street fairs, public art projects - that bring people together in joy, reflection, and celebration. These rituals wouldn't be one-size-fits-all; they'd reflect the diversity of each community's heritage, values, and creativity.

Inclusion as a Non-Negotiable

A world built for belonging is, by definition, inclusive. This means:

- Public spaces are fully accessible for people with disabilities.

- Programming reflects the cultural and linguistic diversity of the population.

- Safety measures protect against harassment and discrimination in both physical and digital environments.

Inclusivity wouldn't be an afterthought; it would be the baseline for every policy and project.

Economic Systems That Reward Connection

Local businesses would be recognized as community anchors, supported by:

- Tax incentives for hosting public events.

- Grants for converting underused spaces into communal gathering areas.

- Partnerships with schools, nonprofits, and cultural groups to provide multipurpose venues.

The economy would thrive not despite connection, but because of it - since connected communities are more resilient, creative, and prosperous.

The Science That Guides It All

Every policy, urban plan, and program would be informed by ongoing research. Governments, universities, and community organizations would share data openly, tracking:

- Rates of reported loneliness.

- Health outcomes linked to connection.

- Participation in community life.

These metrics would shape continuous improvements, ensuring the vision of belonging doesn't stagnate.

Challenges on the Road to Belonging

Even in this optimistic vision, there would be hurdles:

- Balancing privacy with the need for outreach to isolated individuals.

- Avoiding commercialization that turns connection into a luxury service.

- Ensuring small communities aren't overshadowed by big-city models.

But with intentional design and broad commitment, these challenges could be met.

Why This Vision Matters

Loneliness, as we've seen, is more than an emotion - it's a force that shapes health, economics, and the very structure of society. Designing for belonging doesn't just prevent suffering; it actively builds joy, trust, and mutual care into the places we live, work, and gather.

It's a vision where connection isn't an afterthought squeezed into the edges of our lives - it's the fabric our days are woven from.

In Chapter 15, we'll close the book by pulling together everything we've learned, offering a roadmap that blends personal action, community initiatives, and policy change into a unified strategy for ending the loneliness   epidemic.

Chapter 15 – From Isolation to Integration: A Roadmap to a Connected Future

Over the course of this book, we've traveled from the inner workings of lonely brains and bodies to the halls of government, from quiet personal moments of disconnection to sweeping visions of connection-rich societies. If there's one truth that has emerged from every chapter, it's this: **loneliness is not inevitable.**

Yes, it's an ancient human signal - a warning light that flickers when our need for belonging is unmet. But the chronic, widespread loneliness so many feel today is a modern condition, shaped by the way we build our cities, organize our work, design our technologies, and frame our values. That means it can also be reshaped.

This final chapter brings together the key strategies we've explored, offering a roadmap for individuals, communities, organizations, and governments to work in concert toward a future where connection is the norm, not the exception.

Part I – The Individual Level: Rebuilding Personal Webs of Connection

Change often starts with the smallest units - our own daily choices. As we saw in Chapter 11, you don't have to become a social butterfly overnight. The most effective actions are consistent, manageable, and authentic.

Practical starting points:

- Commit to **one intentional social action per day** - sending a message, making eye contact and smiling, joining a neighbor for a short walk.

- Revisit dormant relationships with a low-pressure reconnection ("You crossed my mind today - how are you?").

- Engage in shared activities - volunteering, classes, or group hobbies - where conversation flows naturally.

- Use digital tools as **bridges**, not destinations: aim for online exchanges that lead to in-person or voice-to-voice connection.

The guiding principle: focus on **quality, not quantity**. Two or three deep, reciprocal relationships can do more for your well-being than a large network of shallow contacts.

Part II – The Community Level: Building Local Belonging

Even the most socially proactive person struggles without supportive environments. Communities can create fertile ground for connection through:

- **Third places**: Libraries, cafés, community centers, parks - spaces where people can gather informally without spending much money.

- **Local traditions and events**: Block parties, cultural festivals, storytelling nights, or skill-sharing workshops.

- **Intergenerational programs**: Pairing students with older adults for mentoring, tutoring, or oral history projects.

- **Mutual aid networks**: Neighbors helping neighbors with groceries, childcare, or home repairs, especially in emergencies.

Local leaders - formal and informal - play a vital role here. A neighborhood organizer, a librarian, or a faith leader can often act as a connection "catalyst."

Part III – The Workplace Level: Turning Jobs into Connection Engines

Because work occupies such a large part of adult life, organizations can be either accelerators or barriers to connection. Companies can:

- Create **connection rituals** - weekly check-ins, shared lunches, cross-team projects.

- Ensure managers receive **relational leadership training** so they can spot and address isolation.

- Support **remote inclusion** by funding in-person meetups and designing engaging virtual spaces.

- Align workloads so connection time doesn't become another stressor.

When workplaces treat connection as a performance asset - not a distraction - they see benefits in innovation, retention, and employee well-being.

Part IV – The Policy Level: Governments as Architects of Belonging

As explored in Chapters 13 and 14, governments hold the levers for large-scale change. Effective policies include:

- **Investing in public infrastructure** for connection - parks, plazas, walking paths, community centers.

- Embedding **social connection metrics** in public health surveys.

- Supporting **social prescribing** in healthcare systems.

- Encouraging **pro-connection urban design** and transport planning.

- Regulating digital platforms to promote healthier, less divisive engagement.

Global bodies like the WHO can facilitate cross-country learning, ensuring that successful models - like the UK's social prescribing or Japan's intergenerational housing - are adapted worldwide.

Part V – A Unified Framework: The Connection Ecosystem

When we map these levels together, we see an ecosystem of connection:

1. **Individuals** take daily steps to reach out and reciprocate.

2. **Communities** create inclusive, accessible spaces for interaction.

3. **Workplaces** integrate connection into culture and operations.

4. **Governments** shape environments where connection is easier than isolation.

No single level can solve the problem alone, but together they create **overlapping safety nets** - so that if one layer frays, others can catch us.

Breaking the Cycle: From Disconnection to Momentum

One of the most hopeful findings in loneliness research is that **connection builds on itself**. Just as loneliness can spiral into deeper isolation, reconnection can spiral upward:

- Small positive interactions boost mood.

- Improved mood encourages more social engagement.

- Increased engagement strengthens bonds, leading to more opportunities for positive interaction.

Once momentum builds, it becomes easier to maintain connection than to lose it.

The Role of Culture and Storytelling

While policies and programs matter, so do the stories we tell about connection. If we treat loneliness as shameful, people hide it. If we normalize it as a human experience - and celebrate the courage of reaching out - we create an environment where asking for company is as natural as asking for directions.

Media, arts, and public campaigns can shift cultural narratives, portraying connection not as a perk for the lucky but as a shared responsibility and a basic human right.

The Vision in Practice

Imagine a typical day in a connected future:

- Your morning walk takes you past a community garden where a neighbor waves you over to taste a new tomato variety.

- At work, your team starts the day with a five-minute check-in, sharing personal highs and lows.

- At lunch, you join a free tai chi class in the park, sponsored by the city's health department.

- In the evening, you meet friends for a cooking workshop at the local library's demonstration kitchen.

No single moment is grand, but together, they weave a fabric of belonging.

Why This Matters Now

The urgency is real. Loneliness has been linked to premature death, chronic disease, and mental health crises. But the flipside is just as powerful: social connection has been shown to improve immune function, resilience, and even life expectancy. Every step toward connection is a step toward better health - individually and collectively.

A Call to Action

Ending the loneliness epidemic won't happen overnight, but it also doesn't require waiting for perfect conditions. Here's where to start:

- **As an individual**: Reach out to one person today - just one.

- **As a community member**: Support or start one event that brings people together.

- **As an employer or coworker**: Make space for one non-transactional interaction at work.

- **As a citizen**: Advocate for public investment in spaces and programs that foster connection.

If enough of us act on even one of these levels, the ripple effects will be transformative.

From Isolation to Integration

Loneliness may be a deeply human experience, but so is connection. We are wired for it - biologically, emotionally, and socially. By recognizing this truth and embedding it into how we live, work, and govern, we can move from a world where loneliness is epidemic to one where connection is simply the way things are.

That's the promise of this roadmap: not a utopia, but a society where belonging is built into the structure of everyday life. And in such a world, no one has to face the ache of disconnection alone.

Bibliography

Supporting Research and Contextual References

1. Holt-Lunstad, Julianne, et al. *Loneliness and Social Isolation as Risk Factors for Mortality: A Meta-Analytic Review*. Perspectives on Psychological Science, vol. 10, no. 2, 2015, pp. 227–237.

2. Murthy, Vivek H. *Our Epidemic of Loneliness and Isolation: The U.S. Surgeon General's Advisory on the Healing Effects of Social Connection and Community*. Office of the U.S. Surgeon General, 2023.

3. World Health Organization. *Social Connection as a Global Health Priority: World Health Assembly Resolution WHA77.15*. WHO, 2025.

4. Cacioppo, John T., and William Patrick. *Loneliness: Human Nature and the Need for Social Connection*. W. W. Norton & Company, 2008.

5. Putnam, Robert D. *Bowling Alone: The Collapse and Revival of American Community*. Simon & Schuster, 2000.

6. OECD. *How's Life? Measuring Well-Being*. OECD Publishing, 2020.

7. Office for National Statistics (UK). *Measuring Loneliness: Guidance for Use of the National Indicators on Surveys*. ONS, 2018.

8. OECD. *Beyond GDP: Measuring What Counts for Economic and Social Performance*. OECD Publishing, 2018.

Glossary

Algorithmic Design – The way computer programs (especially on social media) are structured to determine what content users see, often influencing social connection or disconnection.

Belonging – A deep feeling of being accepted, valued, and connected to a group or community.

Chronic Loneliness – Persistent feelings of social disconnection that last for months or years and can negatively affect mental and physical health.

Community Infrastructure – The physical and organizational structures (parks, libraries, clubs, community centers) that support social interaction and community life.

Digital Disconnection – Reduced quality of human relationships caused by overreliance on or misuse of technology and online communication.

Hikikomori – A Japanese term describing individuals who withdraw from social life, often staying at home for extended periods.

Intergenerational Programs – Initiatives designed to bring together people of different age groups for mutual learning and relationship-building.

Minister for Loneliness – A government-appointed official tasked with leading national efforts to reduce loneliness and strengthen social connection.

Psychological Safety – The belief that one can speak, take risks, and be authentic in a group without fear of negative consequences.

Public Health Crisis – A situation that poses significant health risks to a large population and requires coordinated action.

Social Determinants of Health – Social and economic conditions, such as housing, education, and community belonging, that significantly influence health outcomes.

Social Prescribing – A healthcare approach where medical professionals refer patients to community activities or support networks instead of - or alongside - medical treatment.

Third Places – Public spaces that are neither home (first place) nor work (second place) where people can gather and interact informally, such as cafés, parks, or libraries.

Weak Ties – Casual social connections that, while not deeply personal, expand a person's network and sense of belonging.